Fugue With Bedbug

ALSO BY THE AUTHOR

The Quiet

FUGUE WITH BEDBUG

POEMS

ANNE-MARIE TURZA

ANANSI

Published in Canada in 2022 and the USA in 2022 by
House of Anansi Press Inc.
www.houseofanansi.com

House of Anansi Press is committed to protecting our natural
environment. This book is made of material from well-managed
FSC®-certified forests, recycled materials, and other controlled
sources.

House of Anansi Press is a Global Certified Accessible™
(GCA by Benetech) publisher. The ebook version of this book
meets stringent accessibility standards and is available to
students and readers with print disabilities.

26 25 24 23 22   1 2 3 4 5

Library and Archives Canada Cataloguing in Publication

Title: Fugue with bedbug : poems / Anne-Marie Turza.
Names: Turza, Anne-Marie, 1976- author.
Identifiers: Canadiana (print) 20210375620 | Canadiana (ebook)
20210375639 | ISBN 9781487010720 (softcover) |
ISBN 9781487010737 (EPUB)
Classification: LCC PS8639.U79 F84 2022 | DDC C811/.6—dc23

Cover design: Alysia Shewchuk
Text design and typesetting: Laura Brady

House of Anansi Press respectfully acknowledges that the land
on which we operate is the Traditional Territory of many Nations,
including the Anishinabeg, the Wendat, and the Haudenosaunee.
It is also the Treaty Lands of the Mississaugas of the Credit.

 Canada Council   Conseil des Arts   ONTARIO ARTS COUNCIL
for the Arts   du Canada   CONSEIL DES ARTS DE L'ONTARIO
an Ontario government agency
un organisme du gouvernement de l'Ontario

With the participation of the Government of Canada | Canadä
Avec la participation du gouvernement du Canada

We acknowledge for their financial support of our publishing
program the Canada Council for the Arts, the Ontario Arts Council,
and the Government of Canada.

Printed and bound in Canada

For P.

CONTENTS

**

A FALLEN LEAF COVERED THE WHOLE OF A HOUSE

The house was a bungalow size.
And the leaf, a leaf
found in drifts every year, near a tree.

We stood at a window: and could see nothing.

Not a guess or a glimmer.

     We love the dark. It has heard our voice
     and our supplications. We wish. We wish
     to hurt no one. We play piano

     very poorly. In the key of type O negative,
     blood anyone could marry
     to never again be ill.

     What.
     We go to the what and touch it,
     only in thought: *like this.*
     We are doing this all our lives, one of us says.

     It sounds in our heads like good piano sometimes.

     One of us is a binary number.
     And one of us is fog.
     And one of us is a nurse.

We are only ourselves.
There are distinct possibilities.

We work the pedals with whatever limbs
we have. We have failed so far
at everything. *Shh*.

We offer marmalade to one of us
who doesn't know what that is.
And we eat it with a little salt in the dark house.
We do not need rescuing.

WHAT IS THIS? THE FUTUREWORLD?

Same as the afterworld? Adventitious breathing sounds
in both directions. The mind is an interrobang, a zip-filed

mark of kick. Or a distant crackle, actually a chip bag. Off-
target, unfurnished with an air bridge. But this isn't me, I'm not this

venturesome. What is nothingness? I hope to persist somehow
in a radiant 4.5-centimetre ordinary idea belonging to a not-

human future animal. Many similar impossible things are true
already: light in a laboratory twisted into a French braid; or two

quantum whatsits, aloof in space, sharing the same exact existence.

OUR PURPOSE

Our purpose is to husband the colour red.
We are husbands with a pocket in our aprons.
Our aprons are only cloth. And we are faint,
a real individual speck, historical
on the docks of someplace.
Red is the end of the visible range.
Red itself is husband to a myth.
The elbow of one husband
grazes another's throat, and that husband
with a foot in the windfall gait of some further husband,
has in permanence closed his eyes.
We are a clearing for a worthy period of minutes.
A flash something preens in us like a red bird.

❋❋

SEATED FIGURE WITH SNAIL SHELL HEAD

Oil on canvas, c. 2nd millennium

We wore, it's thought, such luncheon shirts
in the Cenozoic era. Held fast at the throat
with folded woven collars, alike to certain
vegetables now extinct, such as cauliflower,
heady and with kindred decorative leaves.
Our forearms were similarly varicoloured
tones welcoming as bathwater, clean scapes
as lightly drawn as the word *utopian*. We had
such vintage laps. All leg and sundry genitals
and we believe we did not pledge any part of us
to clouds, though we did have ample weather
of a size. Certainly we had eyes. It's a swelter
to consider what it means. Were we ever then
outlander, alone in this and that, so many
billion artifacts. To show our minds
we had to paint such scenes.

THE EXIT

I. First Meeting.

The exit was one idea. And I, another.
We pondered in a scratch vernacular.
The coverlet was certainly ours.
It was a lingo of acute angles.

II. But Prior to That, the Problem of Being Human.

By which I mean: facial expressions that were really trees moving
like cultural eyebrows.

III. An Exit Found Me.

It attached itself once I was in the world.

I was here already for some decades pouring pretzels into bowls,
not knowing what an exit was.

Then I was the body.
And a creatured gathering of twos or many threes
became the larger unseen part: an exit I was food for.
Within that larger part, the body, my body, in somnolence.

An exit travelled to my bed and ate of me.

IV. How Many Increments of Time?

My blood was a generous nourishment.
Carried off behind the wall-paint.
I was hurt by the exit's mouth-parts.

V. It Was Really Something.

All material objects. That might house it. I distrusted. Even those unlikely, e.g., inside the radio. For it was a biting exit. And I couldn't find it. It was every hidden place. Not where I could look: its true nowhereity.

VI. Okay.

At night I tightly taped my collar and my sleeves.
The exit bit my face. I washed astringently: nothing doing.
Nor did the oil of pine deter it. I lived in the exit's colony.
What is sleep?

VII. A Song.

Do you know it?
Do you know it?
Do you know how to be rid of it?

The bakers in white paper caps are dancing.
And dogs have torn the sun to hot scraps
littering the yard with little sparks.
That's all the light there is.
Look! Says an only child.
Something moves like future opera.
Large as perfumed nebulas.
Enormous flowers blot out the years.
The bakers in white paper caps are dancing.
Wait, says a small voice, wait,
but that's all the time there is.

⁂

THE AWAKE & SLEEPING YE

The awake and sleeping ye prize different roses.
One has breathed the able hybrid with the thorns.
One eats the sound. One sprints from tree to tree

on a tidal island. A fifth one wears the thirteenth's
shrug. And another, not waking and not sleeping either,
is not anyone on the lee of a known dune.

With nothing else to do, the awake and sleeping ye
trade half a twig: for you, for you.
And more rarely might they gather,

rapping on the lakebed minerals with their knuckles
to signal urgent facts with hands, as divers do.

Some one among them has dispatched another.
They're courteous upon approach. They hold
a necessary knife. Overhead, the blank feet paddle.

DUES IN ARREARS

In Fact. We're compulsory members
of the people's orchestra.
We've not been asked. In the din
there's a face we survey.
The face is a vagary world. And we play
like really good amateurs.

So-and-so many corn kernels later.
Considerable quotidian bus stops.

In Particular. On meeting a snail or any mollusk,
we think of all snails and mollusks
everywhere, trapped in time just as we are.

In Space. We picture the space dog,
strapped in a dog-shaped hold.
We have fashioned from metal
a long-distance ship
installed with a dog heart
hammering madly.

We'll prove it: there's nowhere
animal panic won't go.

In Situ.   The hall itself is tardy: its floor is thereupon.
It's possible to stride almost with
a mauve aplomb across the wooden tiles,
this day, a chipped history of falling
backwards off the roof to surf
in rustling material across the flush canopy
right to the water's edge in a different country.

Though the water is not water: it is pain.
Washing 'round in a high-def fluid galaxy.

Rumble rumble. What the what. What old personage reclines here.
In a robe. Gamely strewn with bold print pineapples.
The lobe of this old one's ear is the most yeared obvious aha
familiar thing I've ever gently touched in space-time.
What do you love most? I blare, bent forward to discharge myself
through major quakes and decades of mosquitoes
      in dissolved parliaments.

Say it clear, so I will know you.
Say it. Say it, old self.

As for me, dear stranger, a white cat is my home thought.
Now you have it. In a cloud forest. Round sums that are her sums
float up. Her leisure had a bright green show. And she was there
in that leisure. I enter my abridging years without her.
Tell me. Just as a century might claim a certain thinker,
will I remain her thinker?

      E. is a soft, composite factor.
      E. samewise has a porous look.
      E. is / is not confounded with.
      E. is dead. E. is a dead factor.
      E.! E.! E.! I call to E.
      E. is running towards me.
      E. does not change, suddenly.

      We need gas laws to understand the language of the lung.
      E.'s lungs are talking. I am also talking. La la la perfusion.
      In attendance: E. and lungs. Myself and lungs.

Set in the aught years of the century, now AWOL years mainly,
ear furnishings of the protagonist cat, resplendent
et cetera and so on.

One can be a person inside other persons
made of previous hours, sounds, the smell of earth:

a small life I am in
rattles over a field of stalks.

E. and I were persons. Eh, what! We were persons
in the time — why not — of twist ties, we were persons
in the time of easy metals, that's saying something.

We were persons together. Take that.
To be a person is to be elsewise
chaseable as noon. That is, a fleeing thing.

Sounds are mortal: yes ❏ no ❏
Hours are mortal, and verbs — certain verbs
keep me from being cumulus. E. is cumulus,

incog in a thermal air mass.
Her tenement did occur. What's more,
time never did astonish her.

She had such beauty guts.
Me, I'm always in a human cupola.

We were persons together.

First person and first person, like filaments,
second person and second person, lit brass lamps.

In the human time of tool-and-die prepackaged cakes.

In whatever were her measurements.

We sit down to study sunlight.
Sunlight has apportioned itself
        in the equal dark
to many present bits of nothing
now aglint, frank silver.

Her white fur with no coloratura.
The gene for that, meaning little

no-word thrown among many
little no-words. I have

my hands to think with. Making almost
the motions of actual bread, moving
as they did in aid of her, though

years beneath the palms have since collected.

Press your forehead to my forehead, older
and older self. I'll show you a meaning

with two animals inside it.

⁂

WHAT HAPPENS IN THE SUBURBS

A tall stair in a neighbour's house,
wallpapered with drawings of further stairs,
and those stairs similarly papered down to an infinity
crawlspace with a cold stream running orange
and tasting of Tang drink mix. In the attic
the varmint animal doing the old jingles
of Burger King, in Pictish. Everywhere
askew, the juniors drop their chins
to loose the one low tone. A daughter
is eaten by a hamster in its ruddy particular,
grown to such a broad incisored angle.
It eats the glossies that tell
how to keep a pen pal, and the daughter
in her unwashed ankle socks.
By now it is a full gleaming mammal
in an ad for a car of great polish
right when the television blinks off.

FORTUNATELY, THERE WERE PLANETS

where we lived in handsome parallel
to ourselves. Otherwise, I could not
have toothed a further boiled egg.

Our bodies were, exactly, thoughts
clinging to the torrent grasses,
supple and iridescent as plastic wrap

but perishable, for no sure reason
aromatic as ellipses —

Our thoughts were long and flexy
penises like those belonging here
to snails, only quick of course in timbre,

and to think, we entered one another.
Yes, we were right for all of it —

Although we amberjacked in time.
Our hooves were ultramodern
lanterns for polyphonic homilies.

We were used to a thundering light,
a beat that tattooed broiling questions —

And there were other worlds, roughly
equal to a tune in town. That is,
when whistling at any altitude, our lungs

were so much lighter than themselves.
Oh, my friends. Whatever was meant by that.
The breakfasts we ate in consequence.

SOME JIMMY UPRISING

Confuse fur for a sound. Strip a roof. Be courteous
to a newt where there is none. Some Jimmy
finishes his coolness to irrational beginnings.
He finishes his coolness for a wound.
The sharp cramp of not being dead,
of giving it or keeping it, whatever *it* this is,
mistaking the air for a known hour
in which to billow humanly.

No one can say for sure what all is affable
as margarine. Maybe it won't serve anything.
But praise the rounds of ping pong and the very paddles,
clamorous and without schedule in gymnasiums.
What else: put on your heels, my Jimmies,
for the multiverse plus plus plus a singing part.
Let no one not in want this time be mallet
to the timpani. And all hairy else. Agree.
You do know what to do with love.

**
**

SLIP MINUTE

1. Inside the slip minute are many kinds of darkness,
    occurring all at once.
    This is true, though almost all the words are wrong —

we have viewed footage from variable sleep,
we scramble up a hill to our interior bodies,
we are in feelings dense as fresh mushrooms,
we have looked as strangers do, like a closed hospital —

        a) The slip minute has no inside.
            Except, perhaps, the inside of an animal.

    A housefly, as it happens, has a timely inside with quick
        informing corners that must seem, to the fly, to be outside

    its body in the slow and geriatric world. The fly sees more,
        sees longer, it seems, in any instant —

we send ideas around a corner,
we are herbs of culture,
we smell the roast infinities —

        Thus. A gust might be

    a long and sculpted era, tremulous with tattered edges.

        Fly darkness

        is the name for this, a gnomic blindness everywhere

only not for flies —

we can say with certainty we were born

in the fly darkness,
in the fly darkness

we have brushed our every hair —

• Plants also may have darknesses.
• In which we cannot clerk.

b) But is it singular, *the* slip minute.

Or, does time have many retrographs.
Many slip minutes, one and one and yet
a separate other, wrackable as arguments,
wherein solid people move

parts of our mutable faces,
and plants are mysterious, yes.

Or else.

Is it us in little pieces, like a sock drawer —

we practise a woodwind embouchure,
we move our tongues against —

• It's plants we want to talk with.
• Time may have different dialects.

c) *Slip minute* is a problem term in brouhaha vernacular.

     Don't blunt it with dull diagrams.
     Don't word word word another word.

         • If plants have darknesses.
         • Is that where plants *are*.

d) *Are* is not for anyone
    who hopes to think on time's fancy maths —

we move our elbows forwardly,
we consider the air in our varied tableaux,
    though that isn't where the moon is, really —

         • Plants, we now believe, have many senses.
         • Of which we have long known nothing.

At intermission:

The subjects sit at a computer.
Its screen shows a bawdy errant line.
When the subjects press the space bar

we learn about the penis in a folk tale
much like this one.[1]

Earlier or later it rains,
it rains in the wayward laboratory.

Even asleep, let's measure it.
Rain is historical.
Plenty of units in rapid eye movement.*

*the units are beagles, the beagles are dreaming

---

1. Pantomimes in spandex leggings leap out from behind the penis. *Ah ha!*, shouts old
Anna, sloshing her beer on the other nonagenarians. In a vast circle, the light collectors
pry bright lids from their barrels. This year the ladder is the very tallest in all of penis
history.

And: the earth has so much matter, its mass
draws down the rounds of water
and they break on the planet's crust;

there is heat and heat-lack, there is vapour,
there are particles of dust;
some atoms of vapour-water, slow. Now
there are clouds where the clouds are.

If rain is the doings of time
and time is a fruiting hollow
and the hollows are many
and the hollows are populous —

we have been here always with these specific jars —

The ory deep sounding of a bell
recalls us now, and a small foolish number
of co-loafers and malingerers.

A ringing length of something.
Wherein one finds a gait or posture.
Meaning in the ad hoc polls,
a person is like a tooth, nearly.
Immersed in a mod bread flour
plus scad-thousand spans of chemistry.
Very like saying. People,

take your troublesome seats.

e) Inside the slip minute are many kinds.
   And the orangutan singular.
   The gaps and funding bodies,
   theories of rolling the fingertips
   over space with a sapient value.

   In the case of *many*, studies show:

   i) nothing is or is not right
   ii) very much —

we are real, our blood has a smell,
we want to know, millimole to litre, what results —

   Just for example, someone reports:

   "I am still doing laundry,
   although I am dead."

   One may ask a grocer
   re: goulash of the hereafter.
   Every salt measure could be fact.

   • Let us reckon on the chorus of plants.
   • The chorus, and one Calico Cactus.

f) It's the pickle of kinds.
   It's the occupied gnarl.
   It's the winshot of a lop.
   Say what.

With a hanker for plainer speak —

we tour the burrs,
we broom on the floating linoleum —

   The slip minute won't give
   one privy word.

   As in: the mirror of feathers
   is the apostrophe.

   As in: "Damn it, Jim, I'm a doctor,
   not an annotated bibliography!"

- The plants of ghazals, E.T.'s plants, plants crushed in the Alps
  by the elephant Surus, the sculpture plants of Las Pozas,
  plants eaten by fictional stevedores, and plants
  of the variously defined Long Nineteenth Century.
- Every living plant of gambit curiosity.

g) Further, are there alternative of's.
   So, there are kinds of darkness.
   And *of* is a soapy wedge
   in some transient water

   so the kinds are clean at the parallel.

   Or *of* is a brassy fixture.
   The slide assembly of a horn.
   With kinds in its rotary valves,

   the slip minute in its bell.

   Or *of* is a gas particulate.
   It means something like a good doughnut

   to a dog, if a dog is smelling it —

we have acted in redolent photoplays,
we are the lake to our exterior want,
we're in a smarting, sharp as triangulars,
we have looked, as fields do, like an open foray —

   So. *In the morning, when we wake,*
   It's time to make the fish cakes.
   A very old song.

   To do a thing, quite practical —

we can say with certainty we have,
we have our every time —

> • Plants also may have certainties.
> • In which we cannot roof.

h) A spectator of the Middle Ages,
    some moment before the year 1050,
    pulled a radish from the sublunary earth
    and swallowed it. A day of given length,
    don't it figure, was certainly involved,
    and the Daikon and the future
    Giant of Sicily in the radish line.

> Regardless *darkness* is literal —

we whistle to the boundary creatures,
we are fragrant noise —

> The hinterlands of dictionaries
> are precisely why

> in the fly darkness,
> in the fly darkness —

we tend our circular glossaries —

> • It's plants we want to think inside.
> • Time may have green imaginaries.

i) The slip minute scholars are so lively.
   When an ostrich is one's steed,
   and one is a gape-mouthed figure

   with a lance and comedian aim
   at the back baldside of another
   who has no breeches. Ha! As

   they say, ink is ink and many such, so
   why be so serious. Have you no cause

   for occurring in the margins
   with a mouldering laughter?

   Be easeful in the slip minute, solemn one.

   The word *occurring* has within it double hooks
   that alter the succeeding sounds —

we mark a turnip with a prize trajectory,
we cormorant a stormy lawn,
we summon a wide berth of coltish singing,
we are a wing of generous distance —

   • Plants, we now believe, have schools of various notice.
   • Of which we have long known nothing.

j) All at once the ice field cracks.
   All at once the loud hum stops.
   We're a system of lymph, and a gallant
   horse-like idea — why not — with a mane
   of hot stuff, turning our oversized head
   when someone remarks: *How good it is
   to see a cloud.* All at once: all at once.

2. The slip minute is a thing — perhaps, of course —
        just like a concertina.

            That is to say: there is lengthening
                    and shortening, there are bellows.

        Eat a carrot, there are centuries.

        Oh, it is more or less

    musical, depending
        on the *pro tem* variables.

            Are there shoes or knuckles,
            are there
            gone people in the earful vicinity
                    doing things in time
                            to sound a provocative rhythm?

            It is human to wonder.

While, in current decades, we amass
more evidence, clouds
don't wonder anything.

Friends, resist.

If you believe this, we'll lose
our precarious why.

> • A plant can learn.[1]
> • A plant can learn.[2]

---

1. Dropped repeatedly from a mild height, a *Mimosa pudica* plant will forgo the defensive curling of its leaves. If then shaken instead of dropped, its leaves will curl. Gagliano, Renton, Depczynski & Mancuso (2014). *Oecologia* 175: 63-72.
2. Ibid. Something inside the slip minute alerts us to our cruelty.

**

THE ONE SNAIL THEORY OF METAPHYSICAL EVENTS

In the first event, I was a gray-wigged general.
Across a lawn, I rode some mother's dingy bicycle.
It was me and the snail, and a lot of credible noise.

In the second event, I did not rightly feature.
But the snail was there.

     For sure:

          the snail is an animal
          of a taxonomic order.

          As much as anyone,
          it belongs in public

          murals of the highest calibre.
          As much as anyone,

          it grazes on a life expectancy.

In the third event I was myself.
I was a calf, also.

The snail did not answer me.

TO WHOM MY HUMAN EMPLOYMENT MAY CONCERN

I understand you are looking for an aspen.

That is, a human body you may at your convenience find
gesturing a yes meant to be an aspen personal to the hands.

For forty years have I been diligent at tasks, variously impossible.

Beckoning to the verge so much invisible water
without a crow ever minding. Now I am able often

to become any number of spaces, stark and vertical

not knowing who is who among me. And as for being
both above and underground, as an aspen grove will be:

daily, I practise this kind of hiding.

I don't care about time.

It's a whale I care about, for I have heard
a whale is a character, sizey and once-
occurring. It cannot be mistaken for blank
heat or space with eyes. The sorry pre-req

for everything I care about is dying.

One specific whale. I'm in the era that is
the 1980s. Time lets me do this. Plum
or nix, my legs are warm. I am outside
the whale, this comforts me. To sleep

I picture the lap of a massive person

also of the '80s. The person has a neon face
at the far end above their chest, lots of blusher
up and up, blurring in the off-zone no one
can see. A lifesize-for-giants '80s person

who will save the decade's whales.

Just like a crimp iron, goodness is corrugating
a strand of hair, the chemical smell of a thing
changing direction in little sharp hot
increments stiff with superhold hairspray:

— good, good, good —

ABSTRACT SELVES

In every class of light, from dove to late
impermanent. Their bodies made of itch

and nerve. They tell an ABC, they have a face,
all tens of years disperse. I'm sure it's just like that:

they can't offer me milk, I have no idea
what cells might work and be theirs,

suddenly it's Donkey Kong cereal together
in a courtyard. Dollars of fog dissolve.

I'll never net the proof. How heft might lift
a private shout. How depth might make their faces

beef, or wink. Give them a mouth to fit
erasure in. And heat, churning the inmost

molecule. Their here is hatched and cross-
hatched. Their zeros move. I must canter

with a little horse, boldly and with special law.
Turn a sudden corner like a capital ell,

come upon a tower, and leap it over.
I don't remember well. From far off

I see myself lift up my terrible face.
Without mass in the least possible part

a chemical thought rises in a puff
so like a breath, it dissipates.

Whereas,

THE SMALL PARTICLES CAN MAKE A HARE
OUT OF CHEMICAL BUNTING

O, CO_2. And other corners
carbon turns to turn into plus
or minus something. Is that hare,
in a car park of energy bonds,

a particular so? *Hares do not bear*
their young underground (needs citation).[1]
Like hare I'm for nests and depressions,
without peer review or a sound

alchemical basis. Where's
hare? Is that hare now?

1.

WE ATE PICKLES TOGETHER, SAYS A DEAD SOMEONE

Someone has made a tiny ladder out of paperclips.
A tiny bird flies through the ladder's rungs.

The bird is a bit of dust.

Only a little bit of dust.

With a stomach.

Where even smaller bits of dust are stirring.

       It is moving, the dust, smaller wakings of dust.

It's not nothing.
Is it, little bird.

. . . you remember.
. . . no matter.
. . . we were happy.

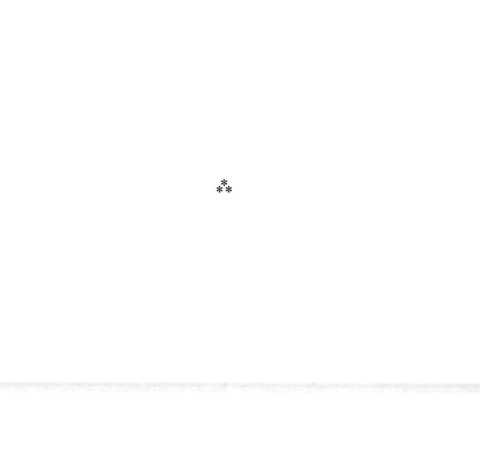

We went into the Cracknarowl.

It was full of cats. No one was surprised
nor expecting it, like crawling inside a fig
and the seeds are turning with fur and inhuman
intentions. What's it mean, the Meaner said.
Those nail scissors were terribly real and
after our necks and our very word. In the end
it was ever further in. We could buy on credit

either anyone's difficult boat,
or one collared rabbit.

We went into the Cracknarowl.

It was loud, there were no little balls of melon,
no bowls anywhere of a nice fruit salad.
A shell-sized bit of window got buffed
with someone's fist, and the view was more bird
than anyone ever wanted. Plus a smell
like licking a rock right out of the fowl's gullet.
And the wind. So we stopped our bootless to and fro

bellowing:
Huh!

We went into the Cracknarowl.

With the Minister in a rowboat riding low
like a bath is a backwards thought: fully
clothed and the bailing can in a modest
shrinking pool of parchedness. To the aft
the sawtoothed zeppelin lions of the falls.
Motor Unit cranking the oars. And the Josher
on the shore in the short boots of the bailaor.

Clap,
clap.

We went into the Cracknarowl.

Cries of infant dogs swelling to venerable howls.
Dressed in our regular selves, we were purpose
dreamside-out, backhanding cricket balls
off the extant tiles with a yell like waking up
ravenous in a hunting lodge, same old encephalons
streaming kilowatts, and a plate of splendid soup
so permanent in the future,

no one born
can drink of it.

Whereas,

THERE ARE TEN TIMES MORE BACTERIAL CELLS
THAN HUMAN CELLS IN THE HUMAN BODY

Let it be resolved:

The brides of my person
are diminutive and few:
I very nearly miss them.
In gowns of flounced organdy.

I meet an irregular shape.
I mistake my wedding for an act.
In the vacuoles of cells
I'm a groom of selfhood.

What's more:

I'm told there's a particle field
that slows the speed of matter

so our forms may coalesce,
and we exist. Marvellous.

Whereon:

Our throat muscles
let us laugh. We say
a glottal word.

None of it works —
you can google it —

without electrolytes
to make things happen.

At last:

We are a child, my cousin,
in the nightdress of a latent year.

The earth has a subscript tilt.
Our limbs are bare.

But:

What have I thought?
A cracked sky would set adrift

soft scraps of foolscap, upon which,
words I needed would half-appear?

If it was only years,
I had them.

But never matched

the torn halves of a longing
given by the air.

THE VISITOR

I've kept a chair and room, as I ought,
where no one sits. It's x o'clock. As if
on stilts, the hour's improbable. It drops
a chancy measurement. Elsewhen and where,

you hammer on the pipes. Blast it: a beller
expulses all arrears. A blouse of water
not clean nor hot but there. Hold on my dear.
I will imagine soon our coarsened hair
and telomeres, our voices elderly.

One of us before the other, disappears.
I don't know who.

APPENDIX I

FALSE ENTRY[A]

Montaigne was fond of coriander, the historian tells me.
You can't get to modernity without coriander.[1]

•

The shoelaces are tied, or they are arranged in Voynich knots,
or they are loose blue lengths, and anyone who is wearing those
shoes knows which it is.[B]

A. *(False Entry.)* Much like the treatises of Herbity, of whom
Sullivan remarked: *Hiſ midday drowſe drummed alwayſ in him a maſſive
diſquiet that could not be anſwered, a vacancy he ruſhed to fill with theorieſ
of appetite and hiſtorical drama.* It is unclear where or when Sullivan
remarked thusly, as the statement is found only in secondary sources.[2]

B. *(Anyone who is wearing those shoes knows which it is.)*
Actually, it is difficult to know — if Velcro is at one's foot, if the word is
eyelet — if one has any socks at all in the passionate service of mystery. For
example, in terms of cake, one asserts: (1) Ingredients have been assembled
in the proper order; (2) The intended cake is of the Black Forest variety. In
eating this cake, one is immediately aware that enzymatic pathways have not
been followed as was intended. One is unsure exactly what one has made.

---

1. "Footnotes have never supported, and can never support, every statement of fact
   in a given work." Anthony Grafton, *The Footnote: A Curious History* (Cambridge,
   MA: Harvard University Press, 1997), 233.
2. In fact, Herbity was a cat of large body and tuxedo markings. This does not render
   the above untrue. In any case, it is movement that interests us. The vertical, the
   horizontal, the historical, and the theatrical. A footnote, for example, is not an
   end-stop.

•

Through assonance, rhythm, placement of the outbuildings, and syllabics, one can read very clearly the unknowable i.e.[C]

•

A form of collective bargaining wherein we agree the *Umwelt* of my aunt is entirely singular. Her sans is no one else's. And her sphere is not water but a foreign element the eye might register in mistake as a liquid colour.[D]

(Remark B. cont'd) Further, a person from the Black Forest informs one that this cake is nothing like the cake found there. We turn to the subject of meaning in sport, also known as the practice of rigorous play. As Jürgen Klopp of Liverpool Football Club proclaims:

> I am not a dreamer.
> I am a football romantic.

We can apply his assertion here to mean it's a King Cake we have made; within it, a figurine is hidden; and we will discover good fortune together, eating cake on the Eve of Epiphany.

C. *(One can read very clearly the unknowable i.e.)* Just so, a pair of psychic snails of the nineteenth century — after a brief time in close proximity touching the other's eye stalks — can be said to act as telegraphs, placed on different continents with the right apparatus and a letter board.[3]

---

3. While this may be veridical, it is agreed most generally that the experiments of Jacques-Toussaint Benoît — involving zinc bowls and lengthy wooden beams assembled into scaffolding, with a copper sulphate glue holding 24 pairs of snails in place (one pair for every letter of the alphabet) — resulted in authentic failure, with dubious transmissions across a horizontal space measuring 10 feet, no more. In this manner the word *gymnase* becomes *gymoate*. What to conclude. In particular, to our knowledge, the Cyrillic or the Hangul alphabet was never tried.

•

The title is *Pastrami*. A multitude of strangers, and every
stranger has a sandwich from which a bite is missing. A map
of that.^F

•

The figure is inverted. Now the plantar aspect of the feet are
the intent. They are dry: the figure's hair is damp.^G

   D. *(Not water but a foreign element the eye might register in
mistake as a liquid colour.)* The concept of the *Umwelt*, as attributed to J. von
Uexküll and T. A. Sebeok, denotes a creature's subjective world. Say, the
Flag-tailed Forest Tumbuloo. If our hands were flat as paper and could fold,
impossibly, into pandimensional instruments of champion knowing, as in the
most sentient and real-seeming origami Flag-tailed Forest Tumbuloo, our
sense of touch would yet remain unequal to the Tumbuloo's *Umwelt*. Of
course, this is a sprightly borrowing of serious terms. Further, be warned:
applied too bluntly to poetics, this paradigm ends in radical loneliness.[4]

---

4. You raise a glimpse in your fist. You shake it, I believe, threateningly. What I liked
   best, always, was not using any words. Worcestershire in such a gust is spelled
   so fancifully.[E]

•

A buggy pushed uphill by a person with binoculars. And inside the buggy there is a spotted dog. The dog is not my psyche.[5]

•

To the left, the lefthand dead who do not know me. To the right, the righthand dead who do not know me.[H]

E. *(Worcestershire in such a gust is spelled so fancifully.)* We're sorry to be ghostly now, to snow in every cold scene. In fact, we aimed to be a hero of real worth: whose mission, in afterthought, was Jell-O, a salad of delicate intent and shimmy; who had a body; who never was without the corresponding pockets; and could nod in fact as much as any grand one.

F. *(Every stranger has a sandwich from which a bite is missing. A map of that.)* Such a map requires the use of ultrasound, also called sonography. In short, sound and echo form the basis of its imagery. (1) Point a sound in the direction of the unknown. (2) Listen for the sound's return. (3) Note how long this takes. (4) Now we know how distant the unknown is. (5) The image of the unknown *is* its distance.[6]

---

5. As Gay notes for the challenge confronting Burckhardt in his conceptualization of the birthing of the Renaissance, "How was he to find modes of expression appropriate to the vast and problematic theme he had chosen for himself?" See Peter Gay, *Style in History* (New York, NY: Basic Books, 1974), 149.
6. A person and a lettuce leaf inside a comet-sized Mason jar, remote in an oddball orbit. The jar is avuncular — so, the glass is familial, lit with remove. Lettuce clothes the person in a cloak of black wilt. Who can then pace tightly in a bantam circle. Who is shouting: *Welcome, my future uncle! Let us garland a heavenly turtle!*

·

From Latin *fuga*, meaning flight. To chase an original idea. And that idea is decamping the present participle.[1]

·

Some terms of being mortal involve pressing oneself through a series of locks so that one is striated while occupying a single active space. One does this in grief.[1]

G. *(They are dry: the figure's hair is damp.)* As in a Mirror Fugue. *Do fa re-re so: os er-er af oD.* In this particular instance, we invite a domestic fruit to become our grade A doppelgänger-mirror. This is speculative fiction, camping with a Red Delicious and some philosophical sugary. Like: for which *why* was the apple ever a canon of pomey radiance?[7]

H. *(To the left, the lefthand dead who do not know me. To the right, the righthand dead who do not know me.)* Among the dead, of course, is Bayle, formulating his clarifications. I, too, "am sorry to have said anything that one might find bad, and I have always been perfectly prepared to remedy in the second edition anything that gives qualms."[8]

---

7. Mirror Fugue: a musical composition following the fugue form, but wherein the identifiable musical phrase that is the fugue's subject occurs in its inverse, played backwards or upside down. Conversely, a False Entry is an incomplete occurrence of the subject, an entry without resolution.
8. See Pierre Bayle, *Historical and Critical Dictionary: Selections*, trans. Richard H. Popkin (Indianapolis, IN: Hackett Publishing, 1991), 398.

I. *(Decamping the present participle / One does this in grief.)*
Grief is a lot of minute golden bodies. Specifically, a colony of pharoah ants.
Intelligence articulates its legs, streaming from a light fixture to track the
pheromone trails through various rooms, right to the body of a phantom hour.
The hour is one in which we can yet murmur to one another, as beings who
are alive together in an era of growing isolative translucency.[9]

J. *(Eliciting a response.)* As a child, I wanted to meet ghosts.
They would happen in the air, a bleach ear to which no one could speak, and
after that a white streak in your hair like the forelock of a memorable horse.

---

9. In entomology, active space refers to a temporal location in which pheromones occur at
   a level of concentration capable of eliciting a response.[J]

The One Snail Theory of Metaphysical Events

Anne-Marie Turza

D. R. Bennett

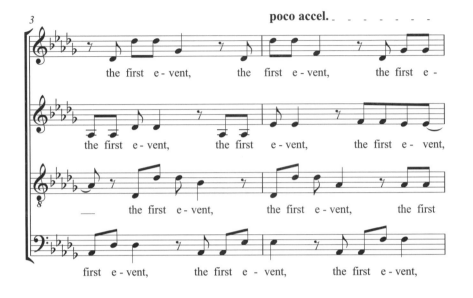

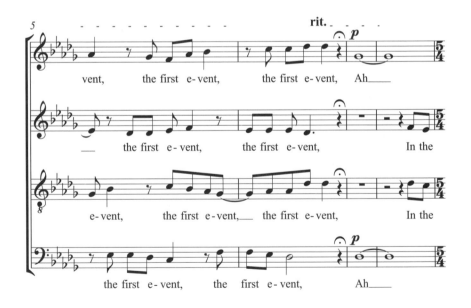

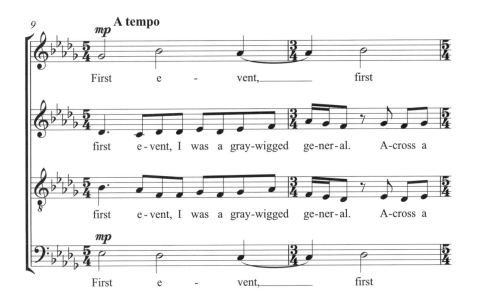

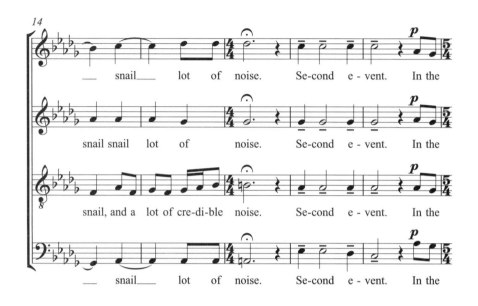

14

snail___ lot of noise. Se-cond e - vent. In the

snail snail lot of noise. Se-cond e - vent. In the

snail, and a lot of cre-di-ble noise. Se-cond e - vent. In the

___ snail___ lot of noise. Se-cond e - vent. In the

19

rit.

se-cond e-vent, I did not right-ly fea-ture. But the snail was there.

se-cond e-vent, I did not right-ly fea-ture. But the snail was there.

se-cond e-vent, I did not right-ly fea-ture. But the snail was there.

se-cond e-vent, I did not right-ly fea-ture. But the snail was there.

For sure: the snail is an an-i-mal of a tax-o-nom-ic or-der.

For sure:

For sure:

For sure:

As much as an-y-one,

As much as an-y-one,

As much as an-y-one, it be - longs in pub-lic mur-als of the high-est

As much as an-y-one,

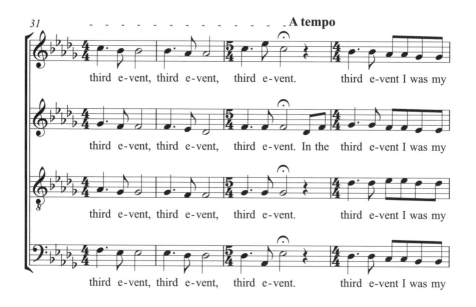

84

self. I was a calf, al - so. The

self. I was a calf, al - so. The

self. I was a calf, al - so. The

self. I was a calf, al - so. The

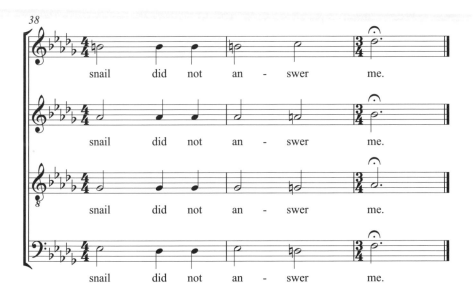

snail did not an - swer me.

snail did not an - swer me.

snail did not an - swer me.

snail did not an - swer me.

ACKNOWLEDGEMENTS

Thank you to the House of Anansi Press. My gratitude to Kevin Connolly for his solicitation and acceptance of this manuscript, to Laura Brady for the text design, and to Alysia Shewchuk for the cover.

Berlin-based composer D. R. Bennett wrote the choral fugato appearing here in Appendix II. Our collaboration and the inclusion of his music in this project are deeply meaningful to me.

Melanie Siebert is a brilliant editor. Her observations and many thoughtful conversations have improved this book in countless ways.

Versions of poems included here have appeared previously in *The Globe and Mail*, *The Malahat Review*, *Arc Poetry Magazine*, and in the chapbook *Slip Minute*. My thanks to Karen Schindler at Baseline Press.

We need gas laws to understand the language of the lung is a beautiful sentence from a lecture on pathophysiology delivered to nursing students by Dr. John T. Fisher at Queen's University in 2014. It appears here in *Down the Corridor a Chair with Wheels Rolls*.

The Canada Council for the Arts and the Ontario Arts Council provided financial support for this project.

DEDICATIONS

Certain friends are central to the landscape and aim of this book. *Fortunately, There Were Planets* and *Comrades of the Good Whyfor* are dedicated to Melanie Siebert, Ali Blythe, and Garth Martens. *Some Jimmy Uprising* is for Garth. *The Awake & Sleeping Ye* is for Ali. *Slip Minute* is for Melanie, with my thanks and affection.

Whereas, the Small Particles Can Make a Hare out of Chemical Bunting is for Sadiqa de Meijer, with good memories of our years together in London and Kingston.

Always, to my brother, Dave: my first and best goal is to write pieces that you might use in your music.

Our Purpose, The Visitor, and *False Entry*[A] are for my partner, Patrick. This book is dedicated to him, with my love.

ANNE-MARIE TURZA is the author of *The Quiet* (House of Anansi Press) and the chapbook *Slip Minute* (Baseline Press). She lives on Vancouver Island.